Read & Dream
STORIES
Magical FOREST
Cat in Boots
Princess
Girl & Frog
100 Fairytales
little prince STORY

BABY Mermaid
Magical FOREST

Z...
Z...
Z...

SWEET
DREAM

ONCE
upon a time...

BOO-KED
Spooky Reader
AFTERLIFE READING
Cursed and Cute
and
Unbothered.

Never stop
DReaMinG

Fairytales
TIME
MR.
in a jungle
fairytales

ABC

BOOK LOVER

BOLD AND EASY COLORING BOOK

54 coloring pages,
featuring Bold and Easy Designs
for Adults, Teens and Kids.

PUBLISHED IN 2025 BY PAGE PUBLICATIONS

BOOK LOVER

BOLD AND EASY COLORING BOOK

Place a piece of paper behind your artwork to prevent bleed through.

this book belongs to